# THE END
# OF
# THE AGE

# THE END OF THE AGE

### WHAT THE BIBLE TEACHES ABOUT THE GREAT TRIBULATION AND THE RETURN OF JESUS CHRIST

## MIKE EVANS

THE END OF THE AGE
Copyright © 2013 by Mike Evans.

All rights reserved. No part of this book may be reproduced, stored in a retrieval system, or transmitted, in any form or by any means—electronic, mechanical, photocopy, recording, or any other—except for brief quotations in printed reviews, without the prior express written permission of the author.

Unless otherwise noted, Scripture quotations are taken from the NEW AMERICAN STANDARD BIBLE®. Scripture taken from the NEW AMERICAN STANDARD BIBLE®, Copyright © 1960, 1962, 1963, 1968, 1971, 1972, 1973, 1975, 1977, 1995 by The Lockman Foundation. Used by permission.

Scripture quotations marked NIV are taken from THE HOLY BIBLE, NEW INTERNATIONAL VERSION®, NIV® Copyright © 1973, 1978, 1984, 2011 by Biblica, Inc.® Used by permission. All rights reserved worldwide.

ISBN 978-0-615-88847-7

# Contents

Introduction     9

**Part 1: Selected Passages from the Old Testament**

1: Daniel 2 and Daniel 7     15

2: Daniel 8     19

3: Daniel 9     23

4: Daniel 11 and Daniel 12     31

5: Zechariah     35

**Part 2: Selected Passages from the New Testament**

6: Matthew, Mark and Luke     41

7: Romans and First Corinthians     45

8: First Thessalonians     47

# Contents

| | |
|---|---|
| 9: Second Thessalonians | 51 |

## Part 3: The Book of Revelation

| | |
|---|---|
| 10: The Dragon, Three Beasts and a Harlot | 57 |
| 11: The Seals, Trumpets and Bowls (1) | 67 |
| 12: The Seals, Trumpets and Bowls (2) | 71 |
| 13: The Two Witnesses and the Woman | 81 |
| 14: The Thousand Years and After | 87 |

## Part 4: Exposition of Old Testament Prophecies

| | |
|---|---|
| 15: Zechariah 14 | 93 |
| 16: Ezekiel 37 Through Ezekiel 39 | 97 |

# Introduction

The Old Testament Scriptures are clear that there is a period of time coming at the end of this present age that will be a time of great distress. The Old Testament is also clear that this time of great distress will be put to an end by the Lord, who will descend from heaven and begin to reign as king over the earth. He will reign from the holy city, Jerusalem.

One passage in particular that speaks of the end of the age is Daniel 11:36-12:4. Daniel 11:21-35 prophesies the actions of a "king of the North" who was yet to come in the days of Daniel the prophet. Daniel 11:35 says that the end time is still to come at the appointed time. The next verse begins to prophesy about the end time. Daniel 11:36-45 describes the character and the actions of the end time "king of the North." Then, Daniel 12:1 promises, "at that time Michael, the great prince who stands guard over the sons of your people, will arise. And there will be a time of distress such as never occurred since there was a nation until that time; and at that time your people, everyone who is found written in the book, will be rescued" (Dan. 12:1). Thus the Lord will rescue his people at the end of the period of great distress. At that time

# Introduction

many people will rise up from out of their graves, and they will live forever (Dan. 12:2).

Zechariah 14 also tells of a time of great distress. This passage of Scripture says that the Lord himself will gather all the nations against Jerusalem (Zech. 14:2). But then on "a unique day which is known to the Lord" (Zech. 14:7) the Lord himself will come and fight against these nations that have gathered against Jerusalem (Zech. 14:3). From that day on, the Lord himself "will be king over all the earth" (Zech. 14:9). The survivors of the nations that went against Jerusalem will go to Jerusalem to worship the Lord (Zech. 14:16). If a nation does not go up to Jerusalem to worship the Lord, that nation will be punished (Zech. 14:17-19).

The New Testament Scriptures reaffirm the coming of the period of great distress that is to come at the end of the age. The New Testament also reaffirms that this period of distress will end when the Lord himself will descend to the earth and begin to reign as king over all the earth.

In Matthew, Mark and Luke, the Lord Jesus Christ teaches people concerning the time of distress that will come at the end of the age (Matt. 24:15-31; Mark 13:14-27; Luke 21:20-28). The time of distress will end with Jesus' return to earth from heaven on the day of the Lord. The coming of the Lord in the sky will be visible just as lightning is visible (Matt. 24:27, 30; Mark 13:26; Luke 21:27).

In 1 Thessalonians, Paul assures his readers that while the day of the Lord will come like a thief in the night upon those who live in darkness, it will not overcome believers like a thief, for believers "are all sons of light and sons of day" (1

# Introduction

Thess. 5:5). Then, in 2 Thessalonians, Paul warns believers not to be deceived "with regard to the coming of our Lord Jesus Christ and our gathering together to Him" (2 Thess. 2:1). For, the day of the coming of our Lord Jesus Christ, the day of the Lord, will not come until after the apostasy and the revealing of the man of lawlessness (2 Thess. 2:2-4).

The apostle Paul also reaffirms the coming of the glorious time that is to follow the day of the Lord, the time during which the Lord Jesus Christ will reign over the earth. In 1 Corinthians, Paul says, "For as in Adam all die, so also in Christ all will be made alive. But each in his own order: Christ the first fruits, after that those who are Christ's at His coming, then comes the end, when He hands over the kingdom to the God and Father, when He has abolished all rule and all authority and power. For He must reign until He has put all His enemies under His feet" (1 Cor. 15:22-25). Thus, when Christ returns on the day of the Lord, all those who believed in him will be made alive and Christ will reign "until He has put all His enemies under His feet." There will be a period of time between the return of Christ and the final judgment, during which there are still unbelievers on the earth.

In Revelation 20, the Lord Jesus reveals to the apostle John that the glorious period of time between the return of Christ and the final judgment will be a thousand years. During the thousand years Satan, the devil, will be bound up in the abyss (Rev. 20:2-3). Satan will not deceive the nations during this time. All of those who are made alive at Christ's coming "will be priests of God and of Christ and will reign with Him for a thousand years" (Rev. 20:6). The final

## Introduction

judgment will come after the one thousand years (Rev. 20:7-15).

This book is about what the Bible, in both the Old and New Testaments, teaches concerning the coming time of distress, the return of the Lord Jesus Christ to the earth, and the reign of Christ as king for the thousand years.  Part 1 discusses several visions and prophecies from the Old Testament.  Most of these visions and prophecies are from the book of Daniel.  Then, there are a couple of prophecies from the book of Zechariah.  Part 2 discusses selected passages from the New Testament, including material from the books of Matthew, Mark, Luke, Romans, 1 Corinthians, and 1 and 2 Thessalonians.  Then, Part 3 is about several visions and prophecies in the book of Revelation.  Finally, Part 4 will examine two passages from the Old Testament, namely, Zechariah 14 and Ezekiel 37-39.

# Part 1

# Selected Passages from the Old Testament

# 1

## Daniel 2 and Daniel 7

In Daniel 2, Nebuchadnezzar king of Babylon has a dream and God miraculously reveals to Daniel the dream and its interpretation. Daniel tells Nebuchadnezzar that the king saw "a single great statue" in his dream (Dan. 2:31). Daniel describes the statue: "The head of that statue was made of fine gold, its breast and its arms of silver, its belly and its thighs of bronze, its legs of iron, its feet partly of iron and partly of clay" (Dan. 2:32-33). The head of gold represents Nebuchadnezzar and his kingdom, Babylon (Dan. 2:38). The breast and arms of silver represent a kingdom that was to arise after Nebuchadnezzar (Dan. 2:39). Persia (or, the Medo-Persian Empire) is the kingdom that arose after Nebuchadnezzar, so the breast and arms of silver represent Persia. The belly and thighs of bronze represent yet another kingdom, a third kingdom. Greece is the kingdom that ruled the earth after Persia, so the belly and thighs of bronze represent the kingdom of Greece.

Now, the legs of iron and the feet of iron and clay are said to represent a fourth kingdom. This kingdom is described in Daniel 2:40-43. It is a kingdom that was to come after the

## 1: Daniel 2 and Daniel 7

third kingdom and crush and break the previous kingdoms in pieces. The Roman Empire is this fourth kingdom that arose after the Greek Empire. Therefore, the legs and feet of the statue represent the Roman Empire.

Now, the statue is not the only thing that Nebuchadnezzar saw in his dream. Daniel reports to Nebuchadnezzar, "You continued looking until a stone was cut out without hands, and it struck the statue on its feet of iron and clay and crushed them" (Dan. 2:34). Miraculously, even though the statue is struck on its feet, the rest of the statue is crushed at the same time, and the wind carries all of the metal away so that not even a trace of it is found (Dan. 2:35). As for the stone itself, Daniel says, "the stone that struck the statue became a great mountain and filled the whole earth" (Dan. 2:35). Daniel explains to the king that the mountain represents a kingdom that the God of heaven himself will set up. He says, "In the days of those kings the God of heaven will set up a kingdom which will never be destroyed, and that kingdom will not be left for another people; it will crush and put an end to all these kingdoms, but it will itself endure forever" (Dan. 2:44). The kingdom that will endure forever is the kingdom of the Lord Jesus Christ and his saints.

The crushing of the statue by the stone does not represent the first coming of Christ, for at his first coming Christ did not put an end to the Roman Empire. Rather, the stone crushing the statue represents what will happen at the second coming of Christ. Since the fourth kingdom, the Roman Empire, is in power when the stone strikes the feet of the statue, it is to be understood that **the Roman Empire will rise again at the end of this age.** Just as the stone strikes the statue on its feet, it is apparent that the feet of iron and clay

## 1: Daniel 2 and Daniel 7

represent the second Roman Empire, the one that is to come at the end of the age, whereas the legs of iron represent the first Roman Empire, the one that was in power when Jesus Christ was born.

In Daniel 7, Daniel himself has a vision. He sees four distinct beasts. The first beast was like a lion, the second beast was like a bear and the third beast was like a leopard. As for the fourth beast, it was different from the previous beasts. It was especially strong and dreadful, and it had ten horns (Dan. 7:7). The fourth beast is so terrifying that it in particular captures Daniel's attention.

Daniel learns that the four beasts represent four kingdoms. As for the fourth beast, with the ten horns, it represents a kingdom from which ten kings will arise. Another king will arise after these ten kings, and he will subdue three of the ten kings. Of this king it is said, "He will speak out against the Most High and wear down the saints of the Highest One, and he will intend to make alterations in times and in law; and they will be given into his hand for a time, times, and half a time" (Dan. 7:25). (A time, times, and half a time means three and a half years.) It is during the reign of this fourth kingdom when the Lord Jesus Christ will return to reign in glory and power with his saints (Dan. 7:9-14, 26-27). Therefore, the fourth kingdom in Daniel 7 is the same kingdom as the fourth kingdom in Daniel 2. So, the first beast, the one that looks like a lion, is Babylon. The second beast, which is like a bear, represents Persia. Then, the third beast, which looks like a leopard, is the kingdom of Greece. Finally, the fourth beast is the Roman Empire. The Roman Empire has come and it has gone, but it will rise again for a short time at the end of this present age.

# 1: Daniel 2 and Daniel 7

Therefore, both the vision of the great statue in Daniel 2 and the vision of the four beasts in Daniel 7 indicated the same sequence of four kingdoms that would dominate the earth. The first of the four kingdoms is Babylon. Babylon was the reigning power when Daniel received these visions. It was represented by the head of gold on the statue and by the lion. The second kingdom is Persia (or, the Medo-Persian Empire). It was represented by the chest and arms of silver and by the bear. Then, the third kingdom is Greece, represented by the belly and thighs of bronze, as well as by the leopard. Finally, the fourth kingdom is the Roman Empire. It is represented by the legs and feet of the statue and by the especially terrifying fourth beast. Both visions indicate that the Roman Empire will be the reigning world power when the Lord Jesus Christ returns in power and glory. Therefore, the Roman Empire will have a second life, so to speak, at the end of the age. Ten kings will arise from this second Roman Empire. Then, another king will arise who will subdue three of the ten other kings. This king will say things against God and will oppress the saints. Then, "his dominion will be taken away, annihilated and destroyed forever" (Dan. 7:26) when the Lord himself comes to the earth to reign. The Lord and his saints will reign over the earth in an everlasting kingdom.

# 2

# Daniel 8

In Daniel 8, Daniel is given another vision (Dan. 8:1-14). This vision features only two beasts: a ram and a male goat. Daniel seeks to understand the vision and Gabriel comes to him to give him understanding (Dan. 8:15-16). Daniel learns that the ram represents the kings of Media and Persia, that is, the Medo-Persian Empire (Dan. 8:20). The male goat is the kingdom of Greece (Dan. 8:21). The vision indicates that Greece would overcome the Medo-Persian Empire. As soon as the male goat, the kingdom of Greece, becomes the dominant world power, the kingdom is broken up into four smaller kingdoms, each one corresponding to one of the cardinal directions of the compass (north, south, east and west; Dan. 8:8, 22; cf. Dan. 11:4). From one of these four smaller kingdoms there comes forth "a rather small horn which grew exceedingly great toward the south, toward the east, and toward the Beautiful Land" (Dan. 8:9). In Daniel 11 it is revealed that the one of the four kingdoms from which this horn comes is **the northern kingdom.** Thus, the small horn that grows exceedingly great in Daniel 8:9 is the power of the king of the North. Several individual men

## 2: Daniel 8

operate under this power; a succession of several kings of the North is prophesied about in Daniel 11.

Each king of the North comes right after the king of the North before him, except for the final king of the North, who is not to come until the end of the age (Dan. 11:35-12:4). It is the cruel reign of this blasphemous final king of the North that is described in Daniel 8:10-12 and 8:23-25. This final king of the North is also the king who comes from the fourth kingdom in Daniel 7, who comes after the ten kings and subdues three of them. Even though he comes from the Roman Empire of the end of the age, he operates under the same power of the kings of the North who had come from the kingdom of Greece. This man is the one whom Paul calls "the man of lawlessness" and "the son of destruction" (2 Thess. 2:3). He "opposes and exalts himself above every so-called god or object of worship" (2 Thess. 2:4; cf. Dan. 7:25; 8:11, 25; 11:36-37).

Thus, the horn that grows "toward the south, toward the east, and toward the Beautiful Land" (Dan. 8:9) comes from the northern kingdom, after the kingdom of Greece is split into a northern kingdom, a southern kingdom, an eastern kingdom and a western kingdom. Daniel observes that this horn from the northern kingdom does some peculiar things. It tramples down the host of heaven, it exalts itself as God, it takes the regular sacrifice away from God and it tramples upon the sanctuary of God (Dan. 8:10-11). Daniel also observes, "on account of transgression the host will be given over to the horn along with the regular sacrifice; and it will fling truth to the ground and perform its will and prosper" (Dan. 8:12). Then, Daniel is told that this vision pertains to a

## 2: Daniel 8

period of 2,300 evenings and mornings, that is, 2,300 days (Dan. 8:13-14).

After seeing this vision of the horn, Daniel seeks to understand the vision (Dan. 8:15). Then, Gabriel is sent to give Daniel "an understanding of the vision" (Dan. 8:16). Gabriel explains to Daniel, "Son of man, understand that the vision pertains to the time of the end" (Dan. 8:17). Daniel then falls asleep, but Gabriel wakes him up and Daniel is made to stand (Dan. 8:18). Gabriel tells Daniel again that the vision pertains to the end, saying, "Behold, I am going to let you know what will occur at the final period of the indignation, for it pertains to the appointed time of the end" (Dan. 8:19). Thus, Gabriel identifies the ram as the Medo-Persian Empire and the male goat as the kingdom of Greece (Dan. 8:20-21). The large horn of the male goat is the first king of the kingdom of Greece, the king who falls as soon as the kingdom of Greece becomes the dominant world power. (This first king conquered the Medo-Persian Empire and made Greece the dominant world power within a very short period of time [cf. Dan. 8:5], over two hundred years after Daniel saw this vision. Today he is known as Alexander the Great. He died in 323 B.C.) Gabriel explains that the kingdom would be split into four smaller kingdoms (Dan. 8:22). Then, in Daniel 8:23-25, Gabriel describes the final king of the northern kingdom, the king represented by the horn in Daniel 8:10-12, the king of the North who will reign at the end of the age (Dan. 11:36-12:4).

Thus, Gabriel tells Daniel "what will occur at the final period of the indignation," at the end of the age. At that time, "A king will arise, Insolent and skilled in intrigue" (Dan. 8:23). He will be empowered by a power from outside of

## 2: Daniel 8

himself. He will destroy many people and he will prosper (Dan. 8:24; cf. Dan. 11:36). This king "will cause deceit to succeed by his influence; And he will magnify himself in his heart" (Dan. 8:25). Furthermore, "He will even oppose the Prince of princes, But he will be broken without human agency" (Dan. 8:25). This vision was to occur a long time off from Daniel's time (Dan. 8:26).

Therefore, Gabriel tells Daniel about the final king who is represented by the horn described in Daniel 8:9. This king is the final king of the North (Dan. 11:36-45). Obviously, this king is an exceedingly wicked man. He will succeed in corrupting the minds of many people. He will also prosper militarily. He will exalt himself above all that is called God. After listening to Gabriel's description of this evil king, Daniel says, "Then I, Daniel, was exhausted and sick for days. Then I got up again and carried on the king's business; but I was astounded at the vision, and there was none to explain it" (Dan. 8:27). Thus, Daniel is astonished. He apparently desires to have a greater understanding of the vision, but he does not get any further explanation right away.

# 3

# Daniel 9

In Daniel 9, Gabriel comes to give Daniel a message and to help him gain understanding of the vision in which Daniel had seen Gabriel previously (Dan. 9:21, 23), that is, the vision in Daniel 8. The message that Gabriel delivers to Daniel is found in Daniel 9:24-27. It is revealed to Daniel that the 2,300 days of the vision of "the final period of the indignation," which "pertains to the appointed time of the end" (Dan. 8:19; cf. Dan. 8:17), is the seventieth and final week of seventy weeks that have been decreed for the people Israel and for the holy city, Jerusalem. The period of 2,300 days is about six years and three and a half months, therefore this seventieth week, as well as each of the other sixty-nine weeks, is a period of seven years. Each of the first sixty-nine weeks is a period of seven whole years, but the seventieth and final week is a time of great distress and tribulation for Israel and for all who will be on the earth at that time. Therefore, the Lord has graciously shortened this seventieth week (Matt. 24:22; Mark 13:20), and so it is shorter than seven whole years. The seventieth week, which is to come at the end of the age, at "the appointed time of the end," is described by Gabriel in Daniel 9:27. By the grace of God, it

# 3: Daniel 9

will be 2,300 days, or about six years and three and a half months, instead of seven whole years.

Thus, Daniel is told that these seventy weeks have been decreed for his people (Israel) and his holy city (Jerusalem). It is with these seventy weeks that God will complete six specific works regarding Israel and Jerusalem. The six works are listed in Daniel 9:24. Then, the seventy weeks are discussed in Daniel 9:25-27. In what follows, Daniel 9:25-27 is discussed in the next four paragraphs, then, Daniel 9:24 will be discussed. That is, the timing of the seventy weeks will be discussed first. Then, there will be an explanation of each of the six things that God will accomplish with the end of the seventy weeks.

Thus, the seventy weeks are described in Daniel 9:25-27. There will be a decree to restore and rebuild Jerusalem. From the time the decree is issued until the coming of the Messiah, there will be seven weeks and sixty-two weeks (and thereby sixty-nine weeks total). The people of Israel could have used this prophecy and should have used this prophecy to predict and anticipate when the Messiah would come. Around the year 458 B.C., the Persian king Artaxerxes issued a decree that provided for the restoration and rebuilding of Jerusalem and the region of Judah. The account of the issuing of this decree is found in Ezra 7, with a copy of the decree written in Ezra 7:12-26. The completion of the rebuilding of Jerusalem around 409 B.C. would have confirmed that the 458 B.C. decree from Artaxerxes in fact had been the decree referred to in Gabriel's message to Daniel. For, each week is a period of seven years, and the city therefore would have been rebuilt after forty-nine years and therefore upon the completion of the first seven weeks.

## 3: Daniel 9

Another sixty-two weeks (that is, seven years times sixty-two, or 434 years) from 409 B.C. would end up at A.D. 26 (there was not a year "0"). Sure enough, Jesus, the Messiah, began his ministry around the year A.D. 26.

Then, in fulfillment of Daniel 9:26, Jesus the Messiah was rejected by the nation of Israel and they executed him by nailing him to a cross. This happened after the sixty-two weeks, about three years after Jesus began his ministry. Then, about forty years later, in A.D. 70, the Romans destroyed the city of Jerusalem and the sanctuary. Of course, the Romans were the people of the fourth beast in Daniel 7, the people of the prince who is to come at the end of the age, at the final period of the indignation. For, even though the prince who is to come is the final king of the northern kingdom of the kingdom of Greece, both Daniel 2 and Daniel 7 indicate that a fourth kingdom (the Roman Empire) would replace the third kingdom (Greece) as the dominant world power. The prince or king of Daniel 8:10-12 and 8:23-25, therefore, will rise up from within the Roman Empire, which will be the dominant world power for a short time at the end of the age.

Finally, in Daniel 9:27, Gabriel further explains the vision of the 2,300 evenings and mornings (Dan. 8:14, 26), which is the seventieth and final week. The seventieth week begins when the prince (or king) makes a covenant with the many of the people of the earth. Yet, "in the middle of the week he will put a stop to sacrifice and grain offering" (Dan. 9:27; cf. Dan. 8:11, 12). Then, Gabriel explains how this evil king or prince "will be broken without human agency" (Dan. 8:25): "and on the wing of abominations will come one who makes desolate, even until a complete destruction, one that is

## 3: Daniel 9

decreed, is poured out on the one who makes desolate" (Dan. 9:27). That is, the Lord himself will pour out a complete destruction upon this exceedingly wicked man.

Thus, these seventy weeks that have been decreed for Israel (that is, the physical descendants of Jacob) and for Jerusalem include many difficult times for the people and for the city, but God will restore both the people and the city with the completion of the seventy weeks. Sixty-nine of the weeks have already occurred; they were the 483 years (that is, seven years times sixty-nine) from around 458 B.C. to around A.D. 26. The seventieth and final week is the final 2,300 days of this present age. It will end with the day of the Lord, the day when Jesus returns in power and glory, which will be followed by a time of glory for God's own people and for the city of Jerusalem and all of the Holy Land.

Concerning these seventy weeks, as it was said above, God will complete six specific works with the completion of these seventy weeks. The works pertain to the people Israel and to the city of Jerusalem. They are listed in Daniel 9:24: "to finish the transgression, to make an end of sin, to make atonement for iniquity, to bring in everlasting righteousness, to seal up vision and prophecy and to anoint the most holy place" (Dan. 9:24). The six works that God will complete are as follows:

1) **To finish the transgression.** The Lord will put an end to the transgressions committed by unbelieving Israel. God does not count the transgressions of believers against them (Ps. 103:12), but he does count the transgressions of unbelievers. It is specifically the transgression of the

## 3: Daniel 9

unbelieving portion of the physical descendants of Jacob that is in view here.

2) **To make an end of sin.** The Lord will eradicate sin from among his holy people. In this age, even those who have been born again, who have been justified by faith and who walk by the Spirit of God, continue to struggle with sin while they are in the world. But once these seventy weeks have been completed, the believers in the Lord Jesus Christ among the physical descendants of Jacob (and Gentile believers, for that matter) will no longer sin, having been perfected soul and body. There will no longer be sin among the people of God.

3) **To forgive iniquity.** Although some translations refer to making atonement or reconciliation for iniquity, what is in view in Daniel 9:24 is not the atoning sacrifice of Jesus Christ on the cross, by which he purchased men with his own blood, but rather the forgiveness of sins that comes by faith in Christ. The same Hebrew verb and noun are used in Psalm 78:38 to celebrate God's forgiving the iniquities of the Israelites when they sinned against him and tested him in the wilderness on their way from Egypt to the promised land. To be sure, it is only the death of Christ on the behalf of sinners that has purchased the forgiveness of sins that comes by faith (2 Cor. 5:15, 21). But, it is **the application of this purchase by Jesus to individual people** that is meant here in Daniel 9:24, not the death of Jesus, which occurred soon after the sixty-ninth week, once for all (Rom. 6:9-10; Heb. 7:27; 9:12; 10:10; 1 Pet. 3:18). After the seventy weeks, all of those among the physical descendants of Jacob whom the Lord has appointed unto salvation will have been saved by faith in the Lord Jesus Christ. They will no longer be held guilty.

## 3: Daniel 9

4) **To bring in everlasting righteousness.** After the completion of the seventy weeks, Jerusalem will never again be trodden under foot by the heathen nations (cf. Luke 21:24). Every person, animal and thing in Jerusalem and Judah will be holy to the Lord (Zech. 14:20-21). The Lord will restore, bless and protect Jerusalem forever once he has brought in everlasting righteousness upon the completion of the seventy weeks.

5) **To seal up vision and prophecy.** At Pentecost, God poured forth his Spirit upon the apostles and other believers. Peter confirmed that this was the outpouring of the Holy Spirit that had been prophesied through the prophet Joel (Acts 2:15-21; cf. Joel 2:28-32). In this age, God graciously gives his Holy Spirit to believers in the Lord Jesus Christ. He also gives many believers the gift of prophecy. Up until the end of the seventieth week, God will continue to give graciously to many members of the body of Christ the gift of prophecy for the edification of the church (1 Cor. 14:3-5). Therefore, many Christians, male and female, young and old, slave and free, Jew and Gentile, will prophesy, dream dreams and see visions until the end of the age. When the Lord Jesus returns on the day of the Lord at the very end of the seventieth week and restores all things, prophecy will no longer be needed (1 Cor. 13:8-12).

6) **To anoint the most holy place.** As promised in Daniel 8:14, the holy place will be restored after the 2,300 days. The evil king who is to come will actually sit in the holy place, intending to reveal himself as God (2 Thess. 2:4). After the seventieth week (that is, the 2,300 days), God will anoint the most holy place and it will never again be profaned by godless men (cf. Zech. 14:21).

## 3: Daniel 9

God will complete these six works with the seventy weeks that he has decreed for Daniel's people (Israel) and the holy city (Jerusalem).

Thus, the vision of the 2,300 days in Daniel 8 pertains to the end of this present age. It is a shortened seven-year period. It is the seventieth week of seventy weeks that have been decreed for Israel and Jerusalem. The first sixty-nine weeks have already occurred; this seventieth and final week is the only one that is still to come. Only God knows when this period of time will come. It is "the final period of the indignation" (Dan. 8:19). At that time a king will arise who "will prosper until the indignation is finished" (Dan. 11:36). This king is the final king of the northern kingdom of the four kingdoms into which the kingdom of Greece was split. He is also the king who arises from the second Roman Empire, after the ten other kings. In the letter of 2 Thessalonians, Paul refers to him as "the man of lawlessness."

# 4

## Daniel 11 and Daniel 12

In Daniel 11, it is reaffirmed that the kingdoms of Persia and Greece would engage in conflict against each other (Dan. 11:2). The first king of the Greek Empire will be mighty (Dan. 11:3). However, "as soon as he has arisen, his kingdom will be broken up and parceled out toward the four points of the compass" (Dan. 11:4). This is the same thing that was foretold by the vision in Daniel 8 (Dan. 8:8, 21-22). This prophecy was fulfilled two hundred years later when Alexander the Great conquered the Medo-Persian Empire and made Greece the dominant world power. Alexander the Great died in 323 B.C., very shortly after making Greece the dominant world power. Then, his vast kingdom was divided into four smaller kingdoms, each one corresponding to one of the cardinal directions of the compass. Thus, there was a northern kingdom, a southern kingdom, an eastern kingdom and a western kingdom.

Daniel 11:5-45 prophesies in great detail about a succession of kings of the northern kingdom. These kings of the North engage in conflicts against kings of the southern kingdom. The kings of the North also cause destruction in the Beautiful Land (that is, Palestine).  This succession of kings of the North was foretold by the vision of the horn in Daniel 8, the "rather small horn which grew exceedingly great toward the south, toward the east, and toward the Beautiful Land" (Dan. 8:9).  Each king of the North comes right after the king of the North before him, except for the final king of the North, the one described in Daniel 11:36-45.  It is this king who performs the evil actions described in Daniel 8:10-12, after the horn has grown from "rather small" to "exceedingly great."  This final king of the North is the man who will make a covenant with many of the inhabitants of the earth, thereby beginning the 2,300 days (Dan. 8:14), which is the seventieth and final week of the seventy weeks decreed for Israel and the city of Jerusalem (Dan. 9:24-27).

Thus, the king of the North of Daniel 11:36-45 will arise at the end of this present age.  He will arise from the Roman Empire that is to come at the end time, after ten kings have already arisen out of the empire (Dan. 7:24-25).  As he is the final king of the North, he will come and operate under the same evil spiritual power as previous kings of the North.  He is arrogant and he speaks against God (Dan. 11:36).  The prophecy says, "He will show no regard for the gods of his fathers or for the desire of women, nor will he show regard for any other god; for he will magnify himself above them all" (Dan. 11:37).  He will prosper until the very end, "with the help of a foreign god; he will give great honor to those who acknowledge him and will cause them to rule over the many, and will parcel out land for a price" (Dan. 11:39).

Then, "At the end time the king of the South will collide with him" (Dan. 11:40).  The king of the South throughout Daniel 11 is the ruler of the southern kingdom of the four

## 4: Daniel 11 and Daniel 12

smaller kingdoms into which the kingdom of Greece was to be split. This southern kingdom is Egypt (Dan. 11:8). Therefore, this king of the South of the end time is the ruler or head of Egypt at the end of the age. He will collide with the king of the North, "and the king of the North will storm against him with chariots, with horsemen and with many ships; and he will enter countries, overflow them and pass through" (Dan. 11:40). The king of the North "will also enter the Beautiful Land, and many countries will fall; but these will be rescued out of his hand: Edom, Moab and the foremost of the sons of Ammon" (Dan. 11:41). He will also conquer and plunder Egypt (Dan. 11:42-43).

The prophecy continues, "But rumors from the East and from the North will disturb him, and he will go forth with great wrath to destroy and annihilate many. He will pitch the tents of his royal pavilion between the seas and the beautiful Holy Mountain; yet he will come to his end, and no one will help him" (Dan. 11:44-45). Thus, the king of the North, the evil king who had come against Jerusalem and who had made it a desolation, will be in northeastern Africa, having conquered Egypt, when he will hear reports that alarm him. He will go back up toward Israel in a rage, to kill and destroy many people. However, even though he will prosper and have success until the very end of the final period of the indignation, he will finally be destroyed. For, on the day of the Lord, the Lord Jesus Christ will return in awesome power and glory. Jesus will rescue his own people. As for the final king of the North, he will be destroyed by the Lord himself. He will suffer a complete destruction under the wrath of the God of heaven and earth.

## 4: Daniel 11 and Daniel 12

Daniel 12 continues the prophecy of Daniel 11, saying, "Now at that time Michael, the great prince who stands guard over the sons of your people, will arise. And there will be a time of distress such as never occurred since there was a nation until that time; and at that time your people, everyone who is found written in the book, will be rescued. Many of those who sleep in the dust of the ground will awake, these to everlasting life, but the others to disgrace and everlasting contempt" (Dan. 12:1-2). Thus, on the day of the Lord, the day when Jesus returns, Jesus will put an end to the time of distress and he will resurrect his own people who sleep in the dust. Those among his people who are still awake at his coming will be rescued.

Finally, Daniel is reminded that there will be "a time, times, and half a time" (that is, three and a half years) of the end during which the saints are given into the hands of the man of lawlessness (Dan. 12:7; cf. Dan. 7:25). He is also told, "as soon as they finish shattering the power of the holy people, all these events will be completed" (Dan. 12:7). Daniel then seeks to gain understanding and he is told, "From the time that the regular sacrifice is abolished and the abomination of desolation is set up, there will be 1,290 days" (Dan. 12:11). That is, there will be 1,290 days from the day that the man of lawlessness and his men set up the abomination of desolation until the day that the power of the holy people is shattered. Then, forty-five days later, at the end of 1,335 days, the righteous will be rescued by the Lord. Those among the believers in the Lord Jesus Christ who are still alive on that final day will be rescued. Believers who have died will be raised up from their graves. Daniel himself is one of the righteous who will be resurrected at the end of the age (Dan. 12:13).

# 5

# Zechariah

This chapter briefly examines two passages in the book of Zechariah, namely, Zechariah 4 and Zechariah 14. Zechariah 4 contains a vision that is referred to in the book of Revelation, specifically in Revelation 11. Then, Zechariah 14 is a passage that speaks of the time of distress that will come at the end of the age. Zechariah 14 also testifies to the physical coming of the Lord to the earth on the last day of the age and his glorious reign as king thereafter.

The vision in Zechariah 4 pertains to the rebuilding of the holy temple in Jerusalem, after it had been destroyed by the Babylonians in the sixth century B.C. When the Jews returned from their exile in Babylon, the Lord called them to rebuild the temple in Jerusalem. At that time, Zerubbabel the son of Shealtiel was one of the leaders who was overseeing the rebuilding of the temple. Through a vision given to the prophet Zechariah, the Lord gave Zerubbabel a word to encourage him in the work of rebuilding. The account of Zechariah receiving this vision is found in Zechariah 4.

# 5: Zechariah

The image that is shown to Zechariah is a golden lampstand. There are also two olive trees by the lampstand, one on each side of it (Zech. 4:2-3). The two olive trees provide golden oil for the lamp (Zech. 4:12). The golden oil represents the Holy Spirit, by whom the people of God would complete the rebuilding of the temple (Zech. 4:6-7). Therefore, the two olive trees are the people of faith of the two houses of Israel. Zechariah is told concerning the two olive trees, "These are the two anointed ones who are standing by the Lord of the whole earth" (Zech. 4:14). One of the olive trees is the house of Judah and the other olive tree is the house of Israel (the house of Israel is also often called the house of Ephraim). The people of the two houses, by the Spirit of the living God, would build the temple and would finish it.

Zechariah had observed that the two olive trees were both in a specific location in relation to the lampstand; one olive tree was to the right of the lampstand and the other olive tree was to the left of the lampstand (Zech. 4:3, 11). The lampstand represents the holy temple in Jerusalem. As the temple in Jerusalem faces east (Ezek. 11:1), the region of Judah, to the south, is on its right side, whereas the region of Israel, to the north, is on its left side. Therefore it is clear that the olive tree on the right side of the lampstand represents the house of Judah and the olive tree on the left side of the lampstand represents the house of Israel.

At the end of the age, during the time of distress that is coming upon the earth, these two olive trees will be powerful witnesses for the Lord Jesus Christ. While the city of Jerusalem is trampled upon by many nations during the final three and a half years of the age (Rev. 11:2; cf. Luke 21:24),

## 5: Zechariah

the two olive trees "will prophesy for twelve hundred and sixty days, clothed in sackcloth" (Rev. 11:3). The believers of the house of Judah and the believers of the house of Israel will be witnesses to the gospel of the Lord Jesus Christ. God will protect them and give them miraculous powers (Rev. 11:5-6).

In Zechariah 14, the prophet speaks of the time that will come at the end of the age when all the nations will come against Jerusalem (Zech. 14:2). The Lord himself will bring this great assault to an end at his glorious return (Zech. 14:3-7). After the Lord Jesus returns, he "will be king over all the earth" (Zech. 14:9). Any of the nations that survive the coming of Jesus in great power and glory will be required to come to Jerusalem each year to worship him (Zech. 14:16). If any of the peoples of the earth do not go to Jerusalem to worship the Lord, they will receive no rain (Zech. 14:17-19).

Therefore, Zechariah 14 clearly tells of a period of time that will begin when the Lord himself returns at the end of this present age, during which the Lord himself will reign as king over all the earth, while there are still unbelievers on the earth. Paul speaks of this period of time in 1 Corinthians (1 Cor. 15:22-25). In the last book of the Bible, the book of Revelation, Jesus reveals to the apostle John that this period of time will be a thousand years (Rev. 20:2, 3, 4, 5, 6, 7).

The prophet Ezekiel also prophesied about this glorious time in Ezekiel 37-39. In this section of Ezekiel's book, he also speaks of the nations from all over the earth, Gog and Magog, coming against Israel after this glorious period (Ezek. 38:1-9; cf. Rev. 20:7-9). Both Zechariah 14 and

## 5: Zechariah

Ezekiel 37-39 are discussed in greater detail in Part 4 of this book.

# Part 2

# Selected Passages from the New Testament

# 6

# Matthew, Mark and Luke

**Matthew 24**

In Matthew 24, the Lord Jesus Christ warns his disciples that many various things must occur before the end of the age. He warns them not to be misled by men claiming to be the Christ (Matt. 24:5). He also warns them that before the end comes there will be wars, rumors of wars, famines and earthquakes (Matt. 24:6-8). The gospel "shall be preached in the whole world as a testimony to all the nations, and then the end will come" (Matt. 24:14).

When the time of the great distress of the end of the age does come, the people of the man of lawlessness will set up the abomination of desolation in the holy place and they will cut off the regular sacrifice (Dan. 12:11). Jesus warns that when that happens everyone who is near, in Jerusalem and Judea, must flee away (Matt. 24:15-20). The day of the setting up of the abomination of desolation and the cutting off of the regular sacrifice will occur in the middle of the seventieth week (Dan. 9:27). Jesus identifies this seventieth week as the time of "a great tribulation, such as has not occurred since the beginning of the world until now, nor ever will" (Matt. 24:21; cf. Dan. 12:1). Referring to this period of time, Jesus says, "Unless those days had been cut short, no life would have been saved; but for the sake of the elect those days will be cut short" (Matt. 24:22). The seventieth week will be 2,300 days, or about six years and three and a half months, instead of seven whole years of twelve months each.

Since the coming of the Son of Man, the Lord Jesus Christ, will be "just as the lightning comes from the east and flashes even to the west" (Matt. 24:27), anyone who claims to be the Christ without having come in that manner is obviously lying. Therefore, Jesus warns not to be deceived by any false Christ or false prophet (Matt. 24:23-26). Such men "will show great signs and wonders, so as to mislead, if possible, even the elect" (Matt. 24:24).

At the end of the great distress, the heavenly bodies will turn dark and the Lord Jesus will appear in the sky (Matt. 24:29-30). "He will send forth His angels with a great trumpet and they will gather together His elect from the four winds, from one end of the sky to the other" (Matt. 24:31). This will be an event that no one on the earth will be able to ignore.

## Mark 13

Mark 13 is very similar to Matthew 24. Jesus warns against those who will come claiming to be the Christ (Mark 13:5-6). Wars, rumors of wars, earthquakes and famines will come before the end of the age (Mark 13:7-8). And, "The gospel must first be preached to all the nations" (Mark 13:10).

When the abomination of desolation is set up, all who are in Judea must flee (Mark 13:14). This will happen at the end of the age, in the middle of the great tribulation, which the Lord has shortened for the sake of the elect (Mark 13:19-20). Jesus warns about those who will come seeking to mislead (Mark 13:21-23). When Jesus does return, it will be obvious. The heavenly bodies will turn dark and Jesus will appear in the sky "with great power and glory" (Mark 13:26). "And then He will send forth the angels, and will gather together His elect from the four winds, from the farthest end of the earth to the farthest end of heaven" (Mark 13:27).

## Luke 21

In Luke 21, Jesus warns his disciples not to follow those who claim to be the Christ (Luke 21:8). He also says, "When you hear of wars and disturbances, do not be terrified; for these things must take place first, but the end does not follow immediately" (Luke 21:9). There will be wars, earthquakes, plagues, famines and signs from heaven that indicate that the end is coming even if it has not yet come (Luke 21:10-11). Before the end of the age, Jesus' disciples will face persecution (Luke 21:12-19).

But, at the end of the age, during the seventieth week described in Daniel 9:27, armies will surround Jerusalem (Luke 21:20) and all who are near must flee (Luke 21:21). Continuing, Jesus explains, "because these are days of vengeance, so that all things which are written will be

## 6: Matthew, Mark and Luke

fulfilled. Woe to those who are pregnant and to those who are nursing babies in those days; for there will be great distress upon the land and wrath to this people; and they will fall by the edge of the sword, and will be led captive into all the nations; and Jerusalem will be trampled under foot by the Gentiles until the times of the Gentiles are fulfilled" (Luke 21:22-24). Thus, many of the Jewish people in Jerusalem will be killed and many will be taken into captivity. Jerusalem will be trampled upon by many nations until Christ returns.

At that time there will be signs in the heavenly bodies and great fear among men (Luke 21:25-26). The coming of the Lord Jesus will be visible and unmistakable (Luke 21:27). Jesus encourages those who would believe that he is Lord and that God raised him from the dead: "But when these things begin to take place, straighten up and lift up your heads, because your redemption is drawing near" (Luke 21:28; Rom. 10:9). Therefore, the appearances of the signs that will occur at the end of the age are to be an encouragement to those who believe in Christ. Christ specifically instructs his disciples against worrying (Luke 21:34). Instead of worry or fear, Christians are called to awareness and to prayer (Luke 21:34-36).

# 7

# Romans and First Corinthians

**Romans 11**

In Romans 11, the apostle Paul explains that God will indeed save every single descendant of Jacob whom he has chosen for salvation. Now, not all who are descended from Jacob are truly Israel (Rom. 9:6). But those whom God has appointed unto salvation will be saved. Thus, Paul says, "all Israel will be saved" (Rom. 11:26). That is, all of the elect from among the physical descendants of Jacob will be saved. By the end of the seventieth week that has been decreed for Israel and for Jerusalem, their iniquities will have been forgiven through faith in Jesus Christ (Dan. 9:24).

**First Corinthians 15**

In 1 Corinthians 15, Paul reaffirms the resurrection of the righteous at the coming of Christ. He also reaffirms the glorious period of Christ's reign that will begin when Christ returns to the earth. Paul explains, "For as in Adam all die, so also in Christ all will be made alive. But each in his own

## 7: Romans and First Corinthians

order: Christ the first fruits, after that those who are Christ's at His coming, then comes the end, when He hands over the kingdom to the God and Father, when He has abolished all rule and all authority and power. For He must reign until He has put all His enemies under His feet" (1 Cor. 15:22-25).

Thus, Paul affirms that Jesus Christ has risen from the dead. When he comes back, at the end of the age, all who belong to him will be made alive. Then, for a period of time, Jesus will reign over the nations of the earth while there are still unbelievers on the face of the earth. In Revelation 20, Jesus reveals to the apostle John that this period of time will be a thousand years (Rev. 20:2, 3, 4, 5, 6, 7). Thus, Jesus and those who are made alive at his coming will reign for a thousand years (1 Cor. 15:25; Rev. 20:4, 6). After the thousand years are completed, death itself will be abolished (1 Cor. 15:26; Rev. 20:14).

Paul therefore affirms the future coming of Christ, the resurrection of the righteous at his coming, and the reign of Christ over his enemies until death itself will be abolished. Paul also affirms that not all believers will die (1 Cor. 15:51). For, when Jesus returns at the last trumpet, the dead who believed in Christ in their lifetime will be raised, and they will be immortal. And, those who are still alive will be made immortal (1 Cor. 15:52).

# 8

# First Thessalonians

In 1 Thessalonians, Paul encourages his brothers in the Lord Jesus regarding those who have died as believers in Christ. Paul explains that just as "Jesus died and rose again, even so God will bring with Him those who have fallen asleep in Jesus" (1 Thess. 4:14). That is, every Christian who has died before Jesus returns will come with Jesus when he returns in power and glory on the day of the Lord. Though the body of a Christian who has died may be buried in the ground, his soul is in heaven with Jesus. When Jesus returns, appearing in the sky, he will bring the souls of these Christians with him. Their souls will be reunited with their bodies and they will be raised up as imperishable and immortal people (1 Cor. 15:52).

Paul wants his readers to know that not only will these believers who have fallen asleep be raised up at the return of Jesus, but "that we who are alive and remain until the coming of the Lord, will not precede those who have fallen asleep" (1 Thess. 4:15). That is, before believers who are still alive at the coming of Jesus are caught up to meet him in the air, "the dead in Christ will rise first" (1 Thess. 4:16). This is a great

## 8: First Thessalonians

comfort to believers are still alive, even at the present. For, the souls of those who have fallen asleep in Jesus are already present with Jesus, in heaven. Furthermore, when Jesus returns, they will come with him and they will be raised up even before we who are still alive are caught up into the air.

Paul also affirms what the Lord Jesus himself had taught concerning his coming, namely, that it will be clear and unmistakable. The apostle writes, "the Lord Himself will descend from heaven with a shout, with the voice of the archangel and with the trumpet of God" (1 Thess. 4:16; cf. Matt. 24:31). Thus, all who live on the face of the earth will know when the Lord Jesus returns. It will be visible and audible. It will be a time of terror for the wicked, but a time of reward for those who are in Christ. All those who have ever died in Christ will be raised imperishable, even those who lived before Jesus was born but who nevertheless believed in the promise of the Christ who was to come (Heb. 11:13). For example, Moses, who "regarded disgrace for the sake of Christ as of greater value than the treasures of Egypt" (Heb. 11:26 NIV), will be raised at the coming of Christ. Daniel the prophet also will be raised on that day (Dan. 12:13). Many righteous men will rise when Jesus returns on the day of the Lord.

Once the dead in Christ have been raised and all believers have been caught up to meet the Lord, we will be with the Lord forever and ever. The Lord Jesus will descend to the earth and he will begin to reign, "For He must reign until He has put all His enemies under His feet" (1 Cor. 15:25). And, all those who had been caught up to meet him will come back to the ground with him and they will reign with him for a thousand years (Rev. 20:4, 6).

# 8: First Thessalonians

Continuing his discussion of the day of the Lord, in 1 Thessalonians 5 Paul exhorts believers to be alert and sober in how they live. For, although the day of the Lord will come as sudden destruction upon those who love wickedness, it will not overtake believers like a thief (1 Thess. 5:2-4). For, believers in the Lord Jesus "are all sons of light and sons of day" (1 Thess. 5:5).

Obviously, once the man of lawlessness rises up from within the second Roman Empire, subduing three of the ten other kings and making a covenant with the inhabitants of the earth, it will be clear that the seventieth week has begun (Dan. 9:27). The Lord will return at the end of the week. Those who understand that Scripture is being fulfilled in the many events of this seven-year period will know that the day of the Lord is coming very quickly. Yet, no one on earth knows when that seventieth week will come. Therefore, Christians are to be aware that those difficult days can come at any time, even though they should not worry about it (Matt. 6:34). Christians are instructed not to worry but to cast their cares upon God himself (1 Pet. 5:7). Instead of fear or worry, Christians are called to watchfulness and to self-control. Paul encourages us, "since we are of the day, let us be sober, having put on the breastplate of faith and love, and as a helmet, the hope of salvation" (1 Thess. 5:8).

# 9

# Second Thessalonians

In 2 Thessalonians, Paul writes again about the glorious coming of the Lord Jesus. When the Lord comes, he will give relief to Christians who have been persecuted, oppressed and afflicted, and yet he will afflict those who afflict his people (2 Thess. 1:3-10). When Jesus comes, he will "be glorified in His saints" and he will "be marveled at among all who have believed" (2 Thess. 1:10). Just as Paul had taught earlier, and as the Lord Jesus himself had taught, the day of the Lord's coming will mean redemption for those who believe, but destruction for those who do evil.

Paul also reminds the Thessalonians that the day of the Lord, the day of "the coming of our Lord Jesus Christ and our gathering together to Him" (2 Thess. 2:1), will not come until "the man of lawlessness is revealed" (2 Thess. 2:3). Apparently, some Christians in Thessalonica had been disturbed by at least one report or rumor that the day of the Lord had already come (2 Thess. 2:2). Had the day of the Lord already come? Had other believers been taken up into the air to meet the Lord while some were not taken? How could anyone be sure that the day of the Lord had not already

## 9: Second Thessalonians

come? Paul's reassurance to his readers is that the day of the Lord will not come until after the man of lawlessness is revealed. This man will be the final king of the North in Daniel 11 (Dan. 11:36-45). "He will exalt and magnify himself above every god" (Dan. 11:36; cf. 2 Thess. 2:4). He will also take "his seat in the temple of God, displaying himself as being God" (2 Thess. 2:4). Paul had told the Thessalonians about the man of lawlessness while he had been in Thessalonica (2 Thess. 2:5).

It is none other than the Holy Spirit of God who restrains the man of lawlessness until the proper time (2 Thess. 2:6). At the appointed time, God will relieve his Holy Spirit of the work of restraining the man of lawlessness (2 Thess. 2:7). Obviously, the Holy Spirit will still be in the world, faithfully doing the work that Jesus said the Holy Spirit would do (John 16:7-15). But he will no longer restrain the lawless one who is destined to come, "the one whose coming is in accord with the activity of Satan, with all power and signs and false wonders" (2 Thess. 2:9). The man of lawlessness will use signs and false wonders to deceive the world. He will also use words and crafty arguments that have an appearance of wisdom, but which are really just a means for him to deceive the people of the earth (Dan. 8:23-25). God himself will allow those who love wickedness to be deceived so that they may be judged (2 Thess. 2:11-12).

Thus, no one needs to be concerned that the day of the Lord has already come. For one thing, the coming of the Lord will be fully noticeable by everyone on the earth. Moreover, the day of the Lord's coming will not come until the man of lawlessness arises and leads many people astray. He will cause great destruction upon the earth and to many

## 9: Second Thessalonians

people. Many people will worship this evil man, but those who know the true God will not worship him. Jesus will destroy him at his coming, at the end of the seventieth week.

# Part 3

# The Book of Revelation

# 10

## The Dragon, Three Beasts and a Harlot

The book of Revelation is "The Revelation of Jesus Christ, which God gave Him to show to His bond-servants, the things which must soon take place; and He sent and communicated it by His angel to His bond-servant John, who testified to the word of God and to the testimony of Jesus Christ, even to all that he saw" (Rev. 1:1-2). There are many prophecies and visions in the book of Revelation. Many of these prophecies and visions pertain to events that will occur during the great tribulation, the final seven years of this present age.

In these many prophecies and visions, there is a dragon and there are also three distinct beasts. The dragon is Satan, the devil (Rev. 12:9). As for the three beasts, two of them are described in Revelation 13 and the other is described in Revelation 17.

The first beast in Revelation 13 John sees coming up out of the sea (Rev. 13:1). John says the beast had "ten horns and seven heads, and on his horns were ten diadems, and on

## 10: The Dragon, Three Beasts and a Harlot

his heads were blasphemous names" (Rev. 13:1). Furthermore, the beast has an overall resemblance to a leopard, feet like those of a bear and a mouth like the mouth of a lion (Rev. 13:2). Thus, the beast that John sees come up out of the sea has features in common with each of the four beasts in Daniel 7. He has ten horns like the fourth beast (the Roman Empire), the likeness of a leopard like the third beast (Greece), feet like that of the second beast (Persia) and a mouth like that of the first beast (Babylon). Therefore, this first beast in Revelation 13 is representative of various world empires. The beast was killed when the first Roman Empire fell. It will come back to life at the end of the age when the second Roman Empire comes to power. People all over the earth will worship the beast (Rev. 13:8), and they will worship Satan, the dragon, because the dragon will give him his authority (Rev. 13:2, 4).

The second beast in Revelation 13 John sees coming up out of the earth. The beast "had two horns like a lamb and he spoke as a dragon" (Rev. 13:11). Thus, this beast presents himself as good and gentle, but his speech is like that of the devil. He deceives the people of the earth with great signs, even making "fire come down out of heaven to the earth in the presence of men" (Rev. 13:13). This beast who comes up out of the earth is the man of lawlessness, "the one whose coming is in accord with the activity of Satan, with all power and signs and false wonders" (2 Thess. 2:9). He is the king who comes from the fourth kingdom in Daniel 7, who comes after the ten kings and subdues three of them, and he is the final king of the North in Daniel 8:10-12; 8:23-25; and 11:36-45. This man tells the people of the earth to make an image to the beast who comes up out of the sea (Rev. 13:14), "And it was given to him to give breath to the image of the beast,

## 10: The Dragon, Three Beasts and a Harlot

so that the image of the beast would even speak and cause as many as do not worship the image of the beast to be killed" (Rev. 13:15).

This beast who comes up out of the earth, the man of lawlessness, also does an evil thing that is especially cruel and arrogant. He makes people get "a mark on their right hand or on their forehead" (Rev. 13:16) so that "no one will be able to buy or to sell, except the one who has the mark, either the name of the beast or the number of his name" (Rev. 13:17). So, the beast who comes up out of the sea has a name and a number. The number is the number of a man and the number is 666 (Rev. 13:18). Now, in all of the Holy Scriptures, there is only one man whose number is 666. Ezra 2 provides a record of the number of men who came back to Jerusalem and Judah from the exile in Babylon. The number of the sons of Adonikam is 666 (Ezra 2:13).

Adonikam is a Hebrew name that means "My lord has arisen." Therefore the number of the beast who comes up out of the sea is 666 and the name of the beast is "My lord has arisen." Obviously, in having this name the beast is recognizing Satan as his lord. It is Satan who gives his authority to the beast (Rev. 13:2, 4). Satan has "arisen" in the reign of the beast in the seven empires he represents. When the many of the inhabitants of the earth take the mark of the beast, they will be acknowledging both Satan and the beast who comes up out of the sea as lord over them. They are worshiping Satan and the beast. They are also worshiping the beast who comes up out of the earth, who "exercises all the authority of the first beast in his presence" (Rev. 13:12).

## 10: The Dragon, Three Beasts and a Harlot

The other beast in the book of Revelation is described in Revelation 17. John sees "a woman sitting on a scarlet beast, full of blasphemous names, having seven heads and ten horns" (Rev. 17:3). So, like the beast who comes up out of the sea, this scarlet beast has ten horns, seven heads and blasphemous names. Yet, this beast who carries the woman is scarlet, whereas the beast who comes up out of the sea resembles a leopard. This scarlet beast, John is told, "was, and is not, and is about to come up out of the abyss and go to destruction. And those who dwell on the earth, whose name has not been written in the book of life from the foundation of the world, will wonder when they see the beast, that he was and is not and will come" (Rev. 17:8). Thus, whereas the first beast in Revelation 13 comes up out of the sea, and the second beast in Revelation 13 comes up out of the earth, this scarlet beast will come up out of the abyss. The scarlet beast is indeed a third beast, distinct from the other two beasts. Yet, he is an image of the beast who comes up out of the sea. He is the image of the beast who comes up out of the sea, the image that the beast who comes up out of the earth tells the people of the earth to make.

Therefore, the man of lawlessness (that is, the beast who comes up out of the earth) tells the people who live on the earth to make an image of the beast who comes up out of the sea. Of course, the man of lawlessness "opposes and exalts himself above every so-called god or object of worship" (2 Thess. 2:4). Thus, even though the man of lawlessness makes people worship the beast who comes up out of the sea (Rev. 13:12), he wants people to make an image to the beast and to worship that image (Rev. 13:14-15). What the man of lawlessness wants is for the world to worship **him.** The man

## 10: The Dragon, Three Beasts and a Harlot

of lawlessness is the image to the beast who comes up out of the sea; he is the scarlet beast.

The scarlet beast is the man of lawlessness, the king who arises from the fourth kingdom in Daniel 7, the king who arises after the ten other kings and subdues three of them (Dan. 7:24). The ten horns on the scarlet beast are those ten kings, and they will rule with him (Rev. 17:12). As for how it can be that the scarlet beast "was" prior to John's day, "is not" in John's day and still "is about to come up out of the abyss and go to destruction," the scarlet beast is the evil spiritual power of the several kings of the North spoken of in Daniel 11. The beast "was" in the succession of kings of the North from the time of the breaking up of the Greek Empire up until the death of Antiochus IV Epiphanes (the king of the North described in Daniel 11:21-35) in 164 B.C. Then, the beast "is not." He "is not" in John's day and he will continue to be "not" until the man of lawlessness comes at the end of the age. At the end of the age, the man of lawlessness will make a covenant with "the many" of the inhabitants of the earth (Dan. 9:27), and the 2,300 days of the seventieth week will begin. The inhabitants of the earth thereby will have made this man into the image of the beast who comes up out of the sea. The scarlet beast, who will come up out of the abyss, will empower the man of lawlessness for 2,300 days, and then he will go to his destruction. The man of lawlessness will be the final king of the North (Dan. 11:36-45) and therefore the final king represented by the horn described in Daniel 8:9.

Now, of the seven heads of the scarlet beast it is said, "The seven heads are seven mountains on which the woman sits, and they are seven kings; five have fallen, one is, the

## 10: The Dragon, Three Beasts and a Harlot

other has not yet come; and when he comes, he must remain a little while" (Rev. 17:9-10). Since the scarlet beast is an image of the beast who comes up out of the sea, the seven heads of the scarlet beast correspond to the seven heads of the beast who comes up out of the sea. There is one head for each of the seven kingdoms represented by the beast who comes up out of the sea. In the history of God's people Israel, the first kingdom who oppressed them was Egypt and the second kingdom was Assyria (Isa. 52:4). Assyria was followed by Babylon (Jer. 50:17). Then, according to the sequence prophesied in Daniel 2 and Daniel 7, Babylon was followed by Medo-Persia, which was followed by Greece, which was then followed by Rome. Therefore, the five kings or kingdoms who had fallen before John's day are Egypt, Assyria, Babylon, Medo-Persia and Greece. The sixth king or kingdom, Rome, is the king who reigns in John's day. Of course, it is this head of the beast who comes up out of the sea that was wounded (Rev. 13:3), when the first Roman Empire fell. Near the end of the age, the wound will be healed and the beast will come back to life. At that time, it is the seventh king who will reign. This seventh king is the second Roman Empire, which will arise for a short time at the end of the age. (Although some translations of Revelation 17:11 imply that the scarlet beast is one of the seven kings, the Greek text says that he is "out of" or "from" the seven.)

Concerning the woman who sits on the scarlet beast, she is called "the great harlot" (Rev. 17:1) and "Babylon the great" (Rev. 17:5). She "is the great city, which reigns over the kings of the earth" (Rev. 17:18). John sees her "drunk with the blood of the saints, and with the blood of the witnesses of Jesus" (Rev. 17:6). The woman sits on seven mountains that

## 10: The Dragon, Three Beasts and a Harlot

correspond to the seven kingdoms represented by the seven heads of the beast. Therefore, the woman sits on the land areas of Egypt, Assyria, Babylon, Medo-Persia, Greece and Rome, as well as the area of the second Roman Empire. That is, Babylon the great, the great city, is the very large land area constituted by these seven areas of the earth.

At the end of the age, during the seventieth and final week (Dan. 9:27), the people of the earth, including the people of the great city, will worship the scarlet beast, the man of lawlessness. The harlot, the great city, will participate with the man of lawlessness in the persecution and the murder of those who hold to the testimony of Jesus. Yet, the man of lawlessness and the ten other kings of his empire "will hate the harlot and will make her desolate and naked, and will eat her flesh and will burn her up with fire" (Rev. 17:16). One example of how they will hate the harlot is the destruction and conquering of many countries within the borders of the great city, including Egypt (Dan. 11:40-43). God Almighty will have "put it in their hearts to execute His purpose" (Rev. 17:17) to judge and punish the harlot. Obviously not every single person within the borders of the great city will be a worshiper of the man of lawlessness, for there will be those within this great land area who fear God and hold to the testimony of Jesus. That is why these people are warned, "Come out of her, my people, so that you will not participate in her sins and receive of her plagues; for her sins have piled up as high as heaven, and God has remembered her iniquities" (Rev. 18:4-5). God will use the scarlet beast and the ten horns to execute judgment against the harlot, and then at the very end she will be judged when the Lord Jesus returns. For, John sees the final judgment and says, "The great city was split into three parts, and the cities of the

## 10: The Dragon, Three Beasts and a Harlot

nations fell. Babylon the great was remembered before God, to give her the cup of the wine of His fierce wrath" (Rev. 16:19). To be sure, God's wrath will come upon all those who take the mark of the beast (Rev. 16:2) and who kill the followers of Jesus Christ (Rev. 16:5-6), but it is clear that Babylon the great will be judged to a particularly great extent.

Thus, the dragon is Satan, the devil. The beast who comes up out of the sea is the power that was behind the six kingdoms of Egypt, Assyria, Babylon, Medo-Persia, Greece and Rome, and that will be behind the second Roman Empire. Each of the seven heads of this beast corresponds to one of these seven kingdoms. The beast who comes up out of the earth is the man of lawlessness (2 Thess. 2:3-10). He is the king who arises from the fourth kingdom in Daniel 7, who subdues three of the ten other kings. He is also the final king of the North (Dan. 11:36-45). He will require people to take the mark of the beast who comes up out of the sea. In Revelation 16:13; 19:20; and 20:10; the beast who comes up out of the earth is referred to as "the false prophet." Also, in each of these three verses, the beast who comes up out of the sea is referred to as simply "the beast."

The scarlet beast, who will come up out of the abyss, is the image of the beast who comes up out of the sea. He is the power behind the horn described in Daniel 8:9, the horn that comes from the northern kingdom of the kingdom of Greece. He will empower the man of lawlessness for the final 2,300 days of this age, that is, for the seventieth week. The woman whom John sees sitting on the scarlet beast is the great city, Babylon the great. This city is the very large land area constituted by the seven large land areas of Egypt, Assyria,

## 10: The Dragon, Three Beasts and a Harlot

Babylon, Medo-Persia, Greece, the first Roman Empire and the second Roman Empire. God will use the beast and the ten horns to bring punishment upon the great city. Then, when the Lord Jesus returns, the great city will drink of the cup of the wrath of God (Rev. 16:19).

# 11

## The Seals, Trumpets and Bowls (1)

In the book of Revelation, there are seven seals, seven trumpets and seven bowls. These are events that will come upon the earth at the end of the age. The seals are presented first, then the trumpets and then the bowls. Now, Jesus returns at the seventh and final trumpet (Rev. 11:14-19; 1 Cor. 15:51-52). So, it is obvious that the events of the seals, trumpets and bowls do not occur in the same order in which they are presented, for the first six bowls will occur before the return of Jesus Christ at the seventh trumpet. Upon reading what is to occur at each seal, trumpet and bowl, it is clear that each seal is followed by the corresponding trumpet, which is followed by the corresponding bowl. For example, the first seal is followed by the first trumpet and the first trumpet is followed by the first bowl. These three constitute a series of related judgments upon the earth. Then, the second seal, the second trumpet and the second bowl will be a series of judgments, and then the third seal, the third trumpet and the third bowl, and so on. The exalted Lord Jesus Christ opens the seven seals because he alone is worthy to do so (Rev. 5:1-5, 9-10). Angels will sound the seven trumpets and will pour out the seven bowls.

## 11: The Seals, Trumpets and Bowls (1)

When Jesus breaks the first seal, John sees "a white horse, and he who sat on it had a bow; and a crown was given to him, and he went out conquering and to conquer" (Rev. 6:2). Of course, this man on the white horse is the man of lawlessness. He is the king of the second Roman Empire (Dan. 7:24-25) and the final king of the North (Dan. 11:36-45). This is the beast who comes up out of the earth and who exercises all the authority of the beast who comes up out of the sea (Rev. 13:12). The many of the inhabitants of the earth have made a covenant with him, and he is now the image of the beast who comes up out of the sea. He is empowered by the scarlet beast who is to come up out of the abyss. This evil king will work to subdue many nations and to spread his empire.

When John hears the first trumpet, he says, "there came hail and fire, mixed with blood, and they were thrown to the earth; and a third of the earth was burned up, and a third of the trees were burned up, and all the green grass was burned up" (Rev. 8:7). Then, the angel with the first bowl pours it on the earth, "and it became a loathsome and malignant sore on the people who had the mark of the beast and who worshiped his image" (Rev. 16:2). Therefore, those who worship the man of lawlessness (for, he is the image of the beast who comes up out of the sea), and who have taken the mark of the beast, will start to suffer for doing so.

Next, Jesus breaks the second seal. This time, John sees a red horse, "and to him who sat on it, it was granted to take peace from the earth, and that men would slay one another; and a great sword was given to him" (Rev. 6:4). Thus, hatred and war is further increased upon the earth. Then, when the second trumpet sounds, a third of the sea becomes blood, a

## 11: The Seals, Trumpets and Bowls (1)

third of the creatures in the sea die and a third of the ships are destroyed (Rev. 8:8-9). When the second bowl is poured out, it is poured out "into the sea, and it became blood like that of a dead man; and every living thing in the sea died" (Rev. 16:3).

Then, the third seal is broken, and a rider on a black horse brings famine upon the earth (Rev. 6:5-6). When the third trumpet is sounded, a third of the rivers and springs of water are made bitter, "and many men died from the waters, because they were made bitter" (Rev. 8:10-11). Then, the third bowl is poured "into the rivers and the springs of waters; and they became blood" (Rev. 16:4).

When Jesus, the Lamb, breaks the fourth seal, John sees yet another horse. It is an ashen, or pale, horse. Its rider has "the name Death; and Hades was following with him. Authority was given to them over a fourth of the earth, to kill with sword and with famine and with pestilence and by the wild beasts of the earth" (Rev. 6:8). When the fourth trumpet is sounded, "a third of the sun and a third of the moon and a third of the stars were struck, so that a third of them would be darkened and the day would not shine for a third of it, and the night in the same way" (Rev. 8:12). Then, the fourth bowl is poured out. It is poured out upon the sun and the sun burns men with intense heat (Rev. 16:8-9).

Thus, these are the first four of seven series of seal, trumpet and bowl judgments that will be executed upon the earth in the final seven years of this age. This period of time is the worst time of distress and tribulation that the earth will ever see (Dan. 12:1; Matt. 24:21; Mark 13:19). It will be horrible. But, it is real and it is coming; it will happen. The

## 11: The Seals, Trumpets and Bowls (1)

things that God will bring upon the earth in these first four series of judgments are clearly very terrible. Yet, the three series of judgments that will come after these first four will be even worse.

# 12

## The Seals, Trumpets and Bowls (2)

The fifth, sixth and seventh series of judgments that will be executed upon the earth in the period of great distress are different from the first four in two significant ways. One way in which they are different is that whereas when each of the first four seals are broken John sees a horse, John does not mention a horse when either the fifth, sixth or seventh seals are broken. The other difference between the first four series of judgments and the final three series of judgments is that the fifth, sixth and seventh trumpets are called, respectively, the first woe, the second woe and the third woe. Thus, after the fourth trumpet is sounded, but before the fifth trumpet is sounded, John says, "Then I looked, and I heard an eagle flying in midheaven, saying with a loud voice, 'Woe, woe, woe to those who dwell on the earth, because of the remaining blasts of the trumpet of the three angels who are about to sound!'" (Rev. 8:13). It is not that the first four trumpets did not bring terrible things upon the earth; they certainly did. Nevertheless, the fifth, sixth and seventh trumpets will bring things that are even worse.

## 12: The Seals, Trumpets and Bowls (2)

Thus, when the fifth seal is broken (Rev. 6:9-11), John sees the souls of Christian martyrs in heaven. They cry out to the Lord, asking him, "How long, O Lord, holy and true, will You refrain from judging and avenging our blood on those who dwell on the earth?" (Rev. 6:10). Then, these people are instructed to wait just "a little while longer" (Rev. 6:11), for the rest of their brothers in Jesus Christ who are to be killed by the inhabitants of the earth must also be killed. Thus, it is not too much longer from the time of the breaking of the fifth seal to the final day when all Christians who have been appointed to martyrdom will have been killed and the Lord Jesus Christ, the Son of Man, will return in awesome power and glory, and will kill those who have killed his people.

After the fifth seal is broken, the fifth trumpet is sounded. The fifth trumpet is described in Revelation 9:1-11. When this trumpet is sounded, demonic locusts are released from the abyss. Now, whereas the first four trumpets directly affected 1) the earth, the trees and the grass, 2) the seas, 3) the rivers and springs, and 4) the sun, the moon and the stars; at this fifth trumpet it is humans who are directly affected. For, the locusts are not permitted to harm the earth or the plants of the earth. Of course, they are not permitted to kill humans either. Instead, they are permitted "to torment for five months" (Rev. 9:5) and they can hurt "only the men who do not have the seal of God on their foreheads" (Rev. 9:4). John says, "in those days men will seek death and will not find it; they will long to die, and death flees from them" (Rev. 9:6). That is, people will want to die because of the torment of these locusts. They will even seek to die, but they will not be able to die. This fifth trumpet is the first of three woes that will come upon the inhabitants of the earth.

## 12: The Seals, Trumpets and Bowls (2)

Now, the torment that begins at the sounding of the fifth trumpet will last for five months (Rev. 9:5, 10). Then, just as the events brought to the earth by the sounding of the seventh trumpet (Rev. 11:14-19) are not necessarily finished before the seventh bowl is poured out (Rev. 16:17-21), for, Jesus returns at the seventh trumpet, so it is apparent that the events brought about by the fifth trumpet are not necessarily finished before the fifth bowl is poured out. That is, just as the seventh trumpet is followed very quickly by the seventh bowl, the same is likely to be the case with each of the first six series of judgments. This means that the suffering associated with the fifth bowl is some of the same suffering associated with the fifth trumpet.

Thus, after the fifth trumpet is sounded, the fifth bowl is poured out. Just as the fifth trumpet is the first trumpet that directly affects humans, so the fifth bowl is poured out "on the throne of the beast" (Rev. 16:10). The first four bowls were poured out on 1) the earth, 2) the sea, 3) the rivers and springs, and 4) the sun. Now, the fifth bowl is poured out directly upon the throne of the beast. John says, "and its kingdom was plunged into darkness" (Rev. 16:10 NIV). The people who belong to the kingdom of the beast will chew on their own tongues because they will be in such great pain, and they will cuss and use all kinds of foul language at God and about God because of the pain. Yet, they will not repent of the evil things that they are doing (Rev. 16:10-11).

In light of the revelation that the saints will be given into the hand of the man of lawlessness for three and a half years (Dan. 7:25) and that the abomination of desolation is set up about three and a half years before Jesus returns (Dan. 12:6-7, 11-12), it is apparent that this fifth series of judgments

## 12: The Seals, Trumpets and Bowls (2)

occurs at the beginning of these final three and a half years of the age. For, the souls of Christian martyrs in heaven are told that the full number of saints who are to be killed are yet to be killed, but will soon be killed. Furthermore, the fifth bowl sends the kingdom of the beast into darkness. It is therefore appropriate to understand the time of this fifth series of judgments as the time at which the man of lawlessness (the scarlet beast) and the ten other kings of his empire (the ten horns on the scarlet beast) will turn against the harlot (Rev. 17:16). They will kill and destroy many of the very people who had worshiped the scarlet beast, which is the image of the beast who comes up out of the sea.

Therefore, it must be around this time that the events described in Daniel 11:40-43 will occur. For, the king of the North, the man of lawlessness, will attack many countries that lie within the borders of Babylon the great. "He will also enter the Beautiful Land" (Dan. 11:41) and he will sit in the holy place in Jerusalem, claiming to be God (2 Thess. 2:4). Since the abomination of desolation will be set up 965 days after the man of lawlessness makes a covenant with the many of the earth (1,335 days before the end of the 2,300 days; Dan. 12:12), the abomination of desolation will be set up only about two years and eight months into the 2,300-day period. So, the fifth series of judgments and the darkening of the kingdom of the beast will come quickly. The man of lawlessness will sweep southward from Europe and will go through Palestine. In Jerusalem, he will sit "in the temple of God, displaying himself as being God" (2 Thess. 2:4). He will proceed to Egypt, to further punish the nation that had come against him (Dan. 11:40, 42-43; the king of the South is the king of Egypt [Dan. 11:8]). The man of lawlessness "will prosper until the indignation is finished, for that which is

## 12: The Seals, Trumpets and Bowls (2)

decreed will be done" (Dan. 11:36; cf. "the final period of the indignation" [Dan. 8:19]). He will have great success in Egypt and in the northern and eastern portions of the African continent (Dan. 11:42-43).

After the fifth series of judgments (that is, the fifth seal, fifth trumpet and fifth bowl), the sixth series of judgments will come. The fifth series, which includes "the first woe" of the three woes, brings much torment to the inhabitants of the earth. The demonic locusts of the first woe were permitted only to torment, not to kill. By contrast, the second woe, which is the sixth trumpet, will bring more death than has ever occurred on the face of the earth. For, at the sixth trumpet, the second woe, at least "a third of mankind" will be killed (Rev. 9:18).

So, at the breaking of the sixth seal, the sixth series of judgments begins. John reports, when he sees the Lamb break the sixth seal, "there was a great earthquake; and the sun became black as sackcloth made of hair, and the whole moon became like blood; and the stars of the sky fell to the earth, as a fig tree casts its unripe figs when shaken by a great wind" (Rev. 6:12-13). Then, men of all kinds, young and old, slave and free, even "the kings of the earth and the great men and the commanders and the rich and the strong," will attempt to cover themselves "in the caves and among the rocks of the mountains" (Rev. 6:15). They will know that their time is very short and that the wrath of God and the wrath of Jesus Christ is imminent (Rev. 6:16-17).

After the sixth seal is broken, the sixth trumpet is sounded and then the sixth bowl is poured out. Again, it is clear in the case of the seventh trumpet and the seventh bowl that the

## 12: The Seals, Trumpets and Bowls (2)

bowl is poured out right after the trumpet sounds. The same is likely the case with the sixth trumpet and the sixth bowl. When the sixth trumpet is sounded, "four angels who are bound at the great river Euphrates" are released, "so that they would kill a third of mankind" (Rev. 9:14, 15). As for the sixth bowl, it is poured out **on the Euphrates River.** The river dries up, "so that the way would be prepared for the kings from the east" (Rev. 16:12). John sees evil spirits going forth from the dragon (Satan), from the beast (the beast who comes up out of the sea) and from the false prophet (the beast who comes up out of the earth, that is, the man of lawlessness). These evil spirits go forth to gather all the kings of the earth to a place in northern Israel, near the city of Megiddo (Rev. 16:14, 16).

Thus, the sixth series of judgments is the most severe series of judgments yet. After the sixth trumpet, which is the second woe of the three woes, four angels will go forth to kill a third of mankind. Even still, it is right after the sounding of the sixth trumpet that the sixth bowl will be poured out and the kings of the earth will be drawn by demonic powers toward northern Israel. Therefore, obviously there will be great destruction and death brought about by the kings of the earth and their armies as they crawl upon the face of the earth toward Israel. Since Israel will be in the center of the great city, Babylon the great, which sits upon the seven land areas that correspond to the seven heads of the beast, the kings of the earth and their armies will be sweeping through Babylon the great as they advance toward Israel. Thus, the destruction brought about by these armies will be especially great within the borders of the great city.

## 12: The Seals, Trumpets and Bowls (2)

Therefore, great destruction will come upon Babylon the great. First, destruction will come at the hand of the scarlet beast and the ten horns (that is, the man of lawlessness and the ten other kings of the second Roman Empire), as well as at the hand of the king of Egypt (Rev. 17:16; Dan. 11:40). Then, further destruction will come as armies from all around the world move toward Israel. As this great destruction comes upon the great city, people all over the earth will mourn for the great city (Rev. 18:9-19). Everyone who will have become rich by trading with the great city will lament and mourn.

As the hordes of nations come toward northern Israel, including kings from all over the earth, the man of lawlessness will still be in northeastern Africa, having conquered Egypt. He will have secured "control over the hidden treasures of gold and silver and over all the precious things of Egypt" (Dan. 11:43). However, he will then hear the report about the kings of the earth gathering toward Israel, where he had previously staked his claim to be God. He will hear about kings and armies having invaded and swept through his empire. Therefore, Daniel 11:44 says, "But rumors from the East and from the North will disturb him, and he will go forth with great wrath to destroy and annihilate many" (Dan. 11:44). Thus, the man of lawlessness will be drawn back up toward Israel.

According to Daniel 11:45, the man of lawlessness, the final king of the North, will settle down in the region that lies between the Dead Sea and the Mediterranean Sea, near Mount Zion. Therefore, the king of the North, who will prosper until the very end of the seven years (Dan. 11:36), will be so strong and powerful that he will manage to take his

## 12: The Seals, Trumpets and Bowls (2)

stand near Jerusalem and stay alive even as the rest of the kings of the earth advance upon Jerusalem (Zech. 14:2). Regardless of how many men might like to kill this man, and regardless of how mighty these men might be, it will be none other than the Almighty King who will kill him. For, the Son of God, the Lord Jesus Christ himself, will slay him at his coming, at the seventh and final trumpet (2 Thess. 2:8; Rev. 19:20).

By coming back up near Jerusalem from Egypt, the man of lawlessness will be fulfilling the prophecy in Daniel 9:27 that "on the wing of abominations will come one who makes desolate, even until a complete destruction, one that is decreed, is poured out on the one who makes desolate" (Dan. 9:27). That is, the man of lawlessness will have set up the abomination of desolation in Jerusalem 1,335 days before the return of Christ. He then will have gone into Egypt. Yet, he will come back up near Jerusalem and he will remain there until the return of the Lord Jesus Christ. As Daniel writes, "He will pitch the tents of his royal pavilion between the seas and the beautiful Holy Mountain; yet he will come to his end, and no one will help him" (Dan. 11:45). God will pour out a complete destruction upon the man of lawlessness.

Thus, while the first four series of judgments bring horrible things upon the earth, the final three series of judgments are more severe, and each one of them is more dreadful than the one before it. Thus, after the sixth series of judgments, in which no less than one third of mankind dies and in which the kings of the earth sweep toward and into the land of Israel, the seventh series of judgments will finally come. The seventh series of judgments will mean redemption for those who believe that Jesus is God, that he

## 12: The Seals, Trumpets and Bowls (2)

died to save men from sin and death, and that God the Father raised him from the dead. At the seventh and last trumpet, all those who have believed in Jesus Christ and have died, even those who lived before Jesus was born but who nevertheless believed in the promise of the Christ who was to come (Heb. 11:13), will be raised from the dead (1 Cor. 15:52). Then, those believers in the Lord Jesus who are still alive at the seventh trumpet "will be caught up together with them in the clouds to meet the Lord in the air" (1 Thess. 4:17). However, for those who have not believed the gospel, the seventh trumpet will be a great terror.

Thus, the seventh seal will be broken, and the seventh series of judgments will have begun. John says, concerning the seventh seal, "When the Lamb broke the seventh seal, there was silence in heaven for about half an hour" (Rev. 8:1). When the seventh trumpet is sounded heaven rejoices, "The kingdom of the world has become the kingdom of our Lord and of His Christ; and He will reign forever and ever" (Rev. 11:15). The seventh trumpet means reward for those who fear God but destruction for "those who destroy the earth" (Rev. 11:18). It is at the seventh trumpet that Christians who have died will be raised and Christians who are still alive will be made immortal. They will all meet the Lord in the air.

Immediately after the seventh trumpet sounds and all believers in the Lord Jesus have been taken up into the air, the seventh bowl will be poured out. The seventh bowl is poured out upon the air and John hears a loud voice pronounce, "It is done" (Rev. 16:17). Having been poured out upon the air, the seventh bowl brings about lightning and thunder (Rev. 16:18). There is also an earthquake and a

## 12: The Seals, Trumpets and Bowls (2)

severe hailstorm (Rev. 16:18, 21). The lightning, thunder, earthquake and severe hailstorm are said to follow the sounding of the seventh trumpet (Rev. 11:19), and therefore the seventh bowl is poured out right after the seventh trumpet sounds. Those who belong to Jesus will be up in the air and therefore they will not be on the ground when the earthquake and the hailstorm come upon the earth. The great city (Babylon the great) will be "split into three parts, and the cities of the nations" will fall (Rev. 16:19).

Furthermore, when Jesus returns he will take both the beast (the beast who comes up out of the sea) and the false prophet (the beast who comes up out of the earth) and they will be "thrown alive into the lake of fire which burns with brimstone" (Rev. 19:20). As for "the kings of the earth and their armies" who had gathered to fight against Jesus, they will be killed by Jesus himself, who will rule forever and ever (Rev. 19:19, 21). The dragon, which is Satan, will be bound up and locked up in the abyss for a thousand years (Rev. 20:1-3).

# 13

## The Two Witnesses and the Woman

In Revelation 11 and 12, there are a couple of visions regarding Israel. The first vision is of two witnesses for Christ. The vision is in Revelation 11:1-13. While the city of Jerusalem is trampled upon by the nations during the final three and a half years of the age (Rev. 11:2; cf. Luke 21:24), these two witnesses "will prophesy for twelve hundred and sixty days, clothed in sackcloth" (Rev. 11:3). The two witnesses "are the two olive trees and the two lampstands that stand before the Lord of the earth" (Rev. 11:4; cf. Zech. 4:14), and therefore they are the believers of the house of Judah and the believers of the house of Israel. (In Zechariah 4 the two houses of the nation of Israel are depicted as two olive trees that provide golden oil for a golden lampstand. This represented the people of the two houses of Israel rebuilding the temple in Jerusalem under the anointing of the Holy Spirit.) Thus, the two witnesses are the two olive trees from the vision in Zechariah 4. They are also two lampstands, because they are witnesses to the gospel of Jesus Christ. (The seven churches in Asia Minor to which the book of Revelation was first written are depicted as seven lampstands [Rev. 1:4, 11, 12, 20].) These two witnesses will

## 13: The Two Witnesses and the Woman

testify to the truth of the gospel of Christ. God will protect them and give them miraculous powers (Rev. 11:5-6). Thus, for the 1,260 days, God will protect the two witnesses from harm and will enable them to complete their testimony.

John observes that after the twelve hundred and sixty days of the two witnesses giving their testimony, "the beast that comes up out of the abyss will make war with them, and overcome them and kill them" (Rev. 11:7). The beast who comes up out of the abyss is the scarlet beast (Rev. 17:3, 8). He is the man of lawlessness, the final king of the North in Daniel 11 and therefore the king in Daniel 8:23-25. This man is also the boastful king who arises from the fourth kingdom in Daniel 7.

Thus, after the twelve hundred and sixty days of the prophesying of the two witnesses, the man of lawlessness will make war against the believers of the two houses of Israel. If the two witnesses begin their prophesying when the abomination of desolation is set up in Jerusalem, when the nations begin to "tread under foot the holy city for forty-two months" (Rev. 11:2), then the man of lawlessness and his men will take thirty days to overcome the power of the two witnesses. For, it was revealed to Daniel that it would be 1,290 days for them to "finish shattering the power of the holy people" (Dan. 12:7, 11). Therefore, the power of the two witnesses, the two houses of Israel, will be overcome 1,290 days after the setting up of the abomination of desolation and the cutting off of the regular sacrifice. The Lord Jesus Christ will return 1,335 days after the setting up of the abomination of desolation and the cutting off of the regular sacrifice (Dan. 12:12), and therefore he will return

## 13: The Two Witnesses and the Woman

forty-five days after the power of the two witnesses is overcome.

Therefore, the beast who comes up out of the abyss will make war against the two witnesses after the 1,260 days. He will overcome them thirty days later. Jesus will come forty-five days after that. But, three and a half days before Jesus comes, the man of lawlessness will finally succeed in killing the two witnesses. This is the man of whom it was foretold that he would have success until the end (Dan. 11:36). Thus, one of his final victories will be the killing of the two witnesses. Now, this does not necessarily mean that the man of lawlessness succeeds in killing every single Christian among the physical descendants of Jacob. But, clearly the massacre will be so great that it will look like they are all dead. John says, "And their dead bodies will lie in the street of the great city" (Rev. 11:8). The great city is Babylon the great (Rev. 17:18). It is the very large land area at the center of the earth, which is constituted by the seven land areas that correspond to the seven heads of the scarlet beast and to the seven heads of the beast who comes up out of the sea (that is, Egypt, Assyria, Babylon, Medo-Persia, Greece, the first Roman Empire and the second Roman Empire). The inhabitants of the earth will celebrate the death of the two witnesses and gloat over their dead bodies (Rev. 11:9-10). Their celebration, however, will be cut short.

For three and a half days, the peoples of the earth will gloat over the dead bodies of the two witnesses. They will refuse to give the two witnesses a proper burial. But, then, the two witnesses will be brought back to life. They will stand up, and then they will be lifted up into the sky (Rev. 11:11-12). This resurrection and lifting up of the two

## 13: The Two Witnesses and the Woman

witnesses will occur on the day of the Lord, when the Lord Jesus returns in great power and glory.

Once the Lord Jesus has returned and has brought back to life not only the believers of the two houses of Israel who lived at the end of the age, but indeed every believing physical descendant of Jacob who ever lived, the two houses of Israel will be joined together to live as one nation in the land of Israel (Ezek. 37:21-22). The Lord Jesus Christ, the son of David, will be their king and prince forever (Ezek. 37:24-25).

The next vision regarding Israel is in Revelation 12:1-17. In this vision, the nation of Israel is portrayed as a woman. John describes what he sees: "a woman clothed with the sun, and the moon under her feet, and on her head a crown of twelve stars" (Rev. 12:1; cf. Gen. 37:9). The woman is protected by God and nourished for 1,260 days (Rev. 12:6), the same number of days as the prophesying of the two witnesses. Satan, the great dragon, will try to kill the woman, but she will be protected (Rev. 12:13-16). Then, in his great anger, Satan will go fight against other believers, "who keep the commandments of God and hold to the testimony of Jesus" (Rev. 12:17).

This vision affirms God's fatherly protection and care for the repentant people of Israel at the end of the age. Just as the Lord Jesus said that when the people living in the land of Israel see the abomination of desolation, they must flee away (Matt. 24:15-20; Mark 13:14-18), so the woman will be taken away to the wilderness at that time (Rev. 12:6, 14). The vision pertains to the final three and a half years of the age. At the very end, when Jesus returns, the dragon will be bound

## 13: The Two Witnesses and the Woman

up and locked up in the abyss for a thousand years (Rev. 20:1-3).

# 14

## The Thousand Years and After

When the Lord Jesus Christ returns, the time of great distress and tribulation will be over. The man of lawlessness will have been put to an end by Jesus himself (2 Thess. 2:8). The beast who comes up out of the sea will have been thrown into the lake of fire (Rev. 19:20). As for the dragon, Satan, he will be bound and kept in the abyss for a thousand years (Rev. 20:2-3). After the thousand years, "he must be released for a short time" (Rev. 20:3).

All those who were martyred for Jesus and indeed all those who died in Jesus up to the time of his coming, even those who believed in Jesus before Jesus was born, will be raised up and they will reign "with Christ for a thousand years" (Rev. 20:4). There will be those among the nations of the earth who did not know Jesus but who survive the coming of the Lord. The prophet Zechariah spoke of these survivors (Zech. 14:16). The Lord Jesus and those who are his will reign over all the nations for the thousand years. Satan will not be able to deceive the nations during this time (Rev. 20:3). These nations will be required to worship the Lord Jesus, the King of Kings (Zech. 14:16-19). They will be

## 14: The Thousand Years and After

punished if they do not. Jesus "must reign until He has put all His enemies under His feet" (1 Cor. 15:25).

Satan will be released after the thousand years (Rev. 20:7). He will once again deceive the nations (Gog and Magog). The peoples all over the earth who have persisted in refusing to know and to love the Lord will be deceived into coming upon Israel and Jerusalem with the intention of attacking the saints and capturing spoil (Rev. 20:8-9). This final attack upon Israel by the nations of the earth was foretold by the prophet Ezekiel (Ezek. 38-39). These nations, however, will not be able even to begin an attack. They will be consumed by fire that will fall down from heaven (Rev. 20:9; Ezek. 38:22; 39:6). Then, Satan himself will be "thrown into the lake of fire and brimstone" (Rev. 20:10). After the armies of Gog and Magog have been destroyed, all of the dead will come to life (Rev. 20:5, 13). They will be judged, "every one of them according to their deeds" (Rev. 20:13). Finally, death and Hades will be done away with in the lake of fire (Rev. 20:14; 1 Cor. 15:26). Also, "if anyone's name was not found written in the book of life, he was thrown into the lake of fire" (Rev. 20:15).

Therefore, every one will be resurrected, both the righteous and the wicked (Dan. 12:1-2; Acts 24:15; Rev. 20:4-5). The righteous will dwell with the Lamb and with God the Father forever and ever. As for the wicked, they will indeed forever be in the presence of the Lamb (Rev. 14:10), but it will be in the lake of fire, where the Lamb will see to it that each one receives the punishment that is due to him. The lake of fire is obviously an extremely harsh place. It was "prepared for the devil and his angels" (Matt. 25:41). Yet, many humans will be tormented there forever and ever

## 14: The Thousand Years and After

because they have sinned against a holy God. God does not take pleasure in the death of the wicked (Ezek. 18:23), and he does not want "any to perish but for all to come to repentance" (2 Pet. 3:9). Only Jesus, God's only begotten Son, can save men from sin and death. Faith in the Son is all it takes. Jesus paid the price.

After the final judgment, heaven and earth will be made new. The new Jerusalem will come "down out of heaven from God, made ready as a bride adorned for her husband" (Rev. 21:2). Thus, the redeemed will live in this holy city, the new Jerusalem, on the new earth. They will live in the presence of God the Father and of Jesus his Son.

# Part 4

# Exposition of Old Testament Prophecies

# 15

## Zechariah 14

Zechariah 14 is an Old Testament passage that prophesies the nations coming against Jerusalem at the end of the age. It also speaks of the Lord himself coming down to the earth to put an end to the attack against Jerusalem. This passage also testifies to the thousand-year period that is to follow the return of the Lord Jesus Christ. To be sure, the specific length of time of one thousand years is not revealed in Zechariah 14. But, after the thousand years of Revelation 20, all those who have not believed in the gospel of Jesus Christ will be put into the lake of fire (Rev. 20:15); there will no longer be unbelievers on the earth. Therefore, Zechariah 14:16-19 must be referring to this thousand-year period, for it speaks of peoples who survive the coming of the Lord but who are not believers.

In Zechariah 14:1, the Lord promises his people that he will restore to them the things that have been taken from them by the other nations. Yet, before this restoration there will be a very difficult time for Jerusalem. The Lord says, "For I will gather all the nations against Jerusalem to battle, and the city will be captured, the houses plundered, the

## 15: Zechariah 14

women ravished and half of the city exiled, but the rest of the people will not be cut off from the city" (Zech. 14:2). Jesus spoke of people being taken captive by these nations in Luke 21:24.

The Lord himself will come and fight against the nations that have gathered against Jerusalem. Of course, there will not be "a fighting chance" for these wicked people who have gathered against Jerusalem and against the Lamb. Those who have gathered in order to make war against the Lord (cf. Rev. 19:19) will be killed by the Lord himself (Rev. 19:21).

When the Lord returns, "His feet will stand on the Mount of Olives, which is in front of Jerusalem on the east" (Zech. 14:4). There will be radical geological events. And, on that day, when the Lord returns, there will be "neither day nor night" (Zech. 14:7). The Lord Jesus Christ "will be king over all the earth" (Zech. 14:9). The land of Israel and the city of Jerusalem will be filled with peace. The people who live there will live in true peace and security (Zech. 14:9-11).

Before the Lord comes, many of the men gathered against Jerusalem will be killed by other men who have gathered there (Zech. 14:13). There will also be a plague that will come upon these men. Specifically, "their flesh will rot while they stand on their feet, and their eyes will rot in their sockets, and their tongue will rot in their mouth" (Zech. 14:12).

Then, during the thousand years, God will graciously bring unbelieving peoples to Jerusalem so that they may worship the Lord Jesus and taste of the goodness of the Lord. Hopefully, there will be those from among these peoples who

## 15: Zechariah 14

will choose to worship the Lord from a grateful, believing heart, and not out of mere obligation. Nevertheless, these nations will be required to go to Jerusalem "from year to year to worship the King, the Lord of hosts, and to celebrate the Feast of Booths" (Zech. 14:16). If they refuse to go to Jerusalem to worship Jesus, they will receive no rain (Zech. 14:17-19). Even though this withholding of rain will be a punishment for the nations who refuse to worship the Lord, even this punishment will be by the grace of God. For, God will be teaching these nations that he is absolutely serious about what he requires of them. After the thousand years, there will be enough people from among all the nations who have refused to love the Lord that "the number of them is like the sand of the seashore" (Rev. 20:8). But, it will not be because the Lord did not make himself known to these people, for he will have revealed his power and glory and goodness to them. Nor will it be due to the deceiving influence of Satan that these people have refused to know the Lord, for Satan will be bound up and unable to deceive the nations during the thousand years.

During the thousand years, every person, animal and thing in Jerusalem and Judah will be holy to the Lord (Zech. 14:20-21). The house of the Lord will be treated as holy (Zech. 14:21). Yes, unbelievers from among the nations will come to Jerusalem to worship the Lord, but they will not be allowed to profane the holy house of the Lord. Thus, Zechariah 14 is an Old Testament passage that affirms the time of distress that is to come at the end of the age, the physical coming of the Lord to the earth on the last day of the age, and the period of the Lord's reign that is to follow.

# 16

## Ezekiel 37 Through Ezekiel 39

In Ezekiel 37, the Lord shows the prophet Ezekiel a valley full of dry bones. The Lord commands the prophet to prophesy life and breath to the bones. When Ezekiel prophesies, the bones come together with sinews on them. The bodies are also covered with flesh and skin. When breath enters the bodies, Ezekiel observes, "they came to life and stood on their feet, an exceedingly great army" (Ezek. 37:10).

Then, the Lord God explains to Ezekiel, "these bones are the whole house of Israel" (Ezek. 37:11). Here, by "the whole house of Israel" is meant the whole nation of Israel, both the house of Judah and the house of Israel. God promises that he will bring his people Israel up out of their graves and back into the land of Israel (Ezek. 37:12-14). Thus, this resurrection of the bones represents the resurrection of the righteous that is to come at the end of the age, on the day when the Lord Jesus Christ returns and rescues his people. And, just as the apostle Paul explains that not all who are descended from Jacob are truly of the people of Israel (Rom. 9:6), so it is only those Israelites who

## 16: Ezekiel 37 Through Ezekiel 39

believed in Jesus Christ who will be raised up from the dead at the first resurrection, before the thousand years. (Of course, Gentiles who have believed in Jesus Christ will also be raised on that day.)

The Lord then gives Ezekiel a second illustration, an illustration that Ezekiel himself will give to the people. The prophet is to take for himself one stick, representing the house of Judah, and another stick, representing the house of Israel (Ezek. 37:16). The Lord tells Ezekiel, "Then join them for yourself one to another into one stick, that they may become one in your hand" (Ezek. 37:17). Ezekiel is to explain to the people, when they ask him what the illustration means, that the Lord will bring all of the people of Israel back to the promised land. In the land, they will be one nation "and one king will be king for all of them; and they will no longer be two nations and no longer be divided into two kingdoms" (Ezek. 37:22). Thus, this prophetic illustration, like the illustration of the bones coming to life, pertains to the first resurrection (cf. Rev. 20:4-6).

After the first resurrection, the believers of the two houses of Israel will live as one nation in the land of Israel, with the Lord Jesus Christ as king over them. As the seventy weeks will have been completed, the people of Israel will no longer transgress in unbelief, they will no longer sin, and their iniquities will be forgiven. The city of Jerusalem and all the land of Israel will be filled with righteousness, prophecy and vision will no longer be needed, and the holy place will be restored and anointed, never again to be defiled. Jesus, the Son of David, will be king over the people for the thousand years and indeed forever and ever. God promises, "And the

## 16: Ezekiel 37 Through Ezekiel 39

nations will know that I am the Lord who sanctifies Israel, when My sanctuary is in their midst forever" (Ezek. 37:28).

Therefore, in Ezekiel 37 the Lord provides two awesome and beautiful illustrations of what he will do for Israel on the day when the Lord Jesus Christ returns, at the end of this present age. He will raise the dead who have believed in him, and he will bring them with him into the land (after these believers have met the Lord in the air). Jesus, the Son of David, will be king over the whole nation of Israel, who will no longer be divided into two houses. The people of Israel will reign with Jesus for a thousand years (Rev. 20:4).

Then, in Ezekiel 38-39, the Lord commands Ezekiel to prophesy concerning Gog and Magog, that is, the nations all over the earth who will have been on the earth during the thousand years (cf. Rev. 20:8). This is an awesome and fearful passage about what the Lord God will do to these peoples at the end of the thousand years, after they have refused to know and love the Lord and his goodness. For, the Lord himself will draw these nations toward Israel (Ezek. 38:4), so that they may be judged. In Revelation, Jesus reveals that God will use Satan to execute his holy purpose. For, Satan, the devil, will be released from the abyss after the thousand years to deceive the nations one last time (Rev. 20:7-8).

Thus, the nations from all over the earth will be deceived into gathering together against Israel, where the people live securely (Ezek. 38:8, 11). The nations will intend to attack the holy people and to take away the great goods and wealth that the Lord will have restored to Israel. But, they will be gathered so that the Lord will execute his great wrath against

## 16: Ezekiel 37 Through Ezekiel 39

them. For, God will send "hailstones, fire and brimstone" upon them (Ezek. 38:22; cf. Ezek. 39:6; Rev. 20:9).

So, the nations will not kill any of the saints and they will not take any spoil. They will fall and die in the sight of all the saints. The saints will burn the weapons of Gog and Magog for seven years and they will take as spoil all the goods that have been left by Gog and Magog (Ezek. 39:9-10). The dead bodies of Gog and Magog will be buried for seven months so that the land may be cleansed (Ezek. 39:11-16).

Of course, soon after Gog and Magog are buried in the land, they will be raised up out of their graves, as will all the wicked who have ever lived, who never repented of their evil deeds and never placed their trust in Jesus Christ, the Son of God. These people will be judged according to what they have done and they will be cast alive into the lake of fire.

It is a sad testimony to the deceitfulness of the human heart and mind, that the nations of the earth, even after seeing the resurrected Lord in Jerusalem, and after seeing the resurrected saints, will decide to come up against Israel after the thousand years. There are many ways that may seem right to the human heart and mind, but only Jesus is the way to God the Father and therefore the way to eternal life. Furthermore, the life that Jesus gives he gives not only in the age to come but also in this age. Jesus says, "Come to Me, all who are weary and heavy-laden, and I will give you rest. Take My yoke upon you and learn from Me, for I am gentle and humble in heart, and you will find rest for your souls. For My yoke is easy and My burden is light" (Matt. 11:28-30).